MW00415724

Comments on
The Book
of

Judges

WITH REFLECTIONS AND EXPLANATIONS
REGARDING THE DEEPER CHRISTIAN LIFE

by
Jeanne Guyon

Judges
All *new* material in this edition
copyrighted by SeedSowers Publishing House
Printed in the United States of America
All rights reserved

Published by The SeedSowers
             P.O. Box 3317
             Jacksonville, FL 32206
             1-800-228-2665

Library of Congress Cataloging - in - Data
        Guyon, Jeanne
        Judges / Jeanne Guyon
        ISBN 0-940232-55-3
        1. Commentary
Visit our exciting website at: www.seedsowers.com

Times New Roman 12 pt.

Books by Jeanne Guyon

Experiencing the Depths of Jesus Christ
Final Steps in Christian Maturity
Intimacy with Christ
Spiritual Torrents
Union with God
Autobiography of Jeanne Guyon

Commentaries by Jeanne Guyon

Genesis
Exodus
Leviticus - Numbers - Deuteronomy
Judges
Job
Song of Songs
Jeremiah
James - First John - Revelation

also

The Life of Jeanne Guyon *(T.C. Upham)*

Publisher's Note:

In this volume Jeanne Guyon did not comment on every verse and chapter. Rather, she selected certain verses. You will also find some passages archaic in language and in spelling.

CHAPTER I.

Judges 1:5   Adonibezek, king of the enemies, is a good type of self-love and greed which when they rule in the heart bring all kinds of trouble. Thus is the heart subject to sin. The Scriptures are always wonderful in their expressions. They say that the Hebrews when fighting against Adonibezek defeated the Canaanites and the Perizzites. This enlightens us on a great truth which is that when we fight self-love and greed, the other enemies become our subjects, because their strength is in this self-love and this greed.

Judges 1:6   As soon as self-love and greed are being attacked by the weapons of Jesus Christ, they soon flee, unable to fight, but we must pursue them in their retreat. If this fearful king survives, he will soon rally enough strength for a second war. It will be more dangerous being unexpected. Besides, the flight of Adonibezek will have made him somewhat strong.

Judges 1:7   Self-love or greed is rightly

compared to this cruel king who cut the toes and thumbs from so many great kings, thus doing away with strength and goodness, and corrupting every good act. . . this shows that there is no pure virtue in a soul, however holy it may appear, while self-love remains. But there will be after its defeat. We must bring him to Jerusalem. This means that we must receive the deathblow from Jesus Christ, in the soul. He alone can bring that death in the soul.

Judges 1:8   What all the people led by Joshua had not dared to do, Judah, type of Jesus Christ, does it beautifully. He attacks Jerusalem, takes, purges and establishes in it the inner people. Jerusalem, sweet abode of peace for the soul which is established in God, only Jesus Christ can bring you souls, lose them in Him, and hide them there. He has acquired this right by his blood.

Judges 1:9   The soul understands that she will never enjoy peace unless all her enemies are vanquished. She also understands that only through Jesus Christ she will be victorious. She begs Him to lead her, and following His flag, she courageously faces her enemies. She first fights against sin, rightly called the Canaanites which were cursed in Canaan, after the flood. The mountain land must be subjected, where pride resides. Then the demon of the South, and also the valley where the enemies are in great number, though they are less to be feared than the first. When pride and fleshly lust, which is the demon of the South are destroyed, the rest is easily conquered.

Judges 1:10　Of all the tribes of Israel, none could be compared to Judah for the victories they won. This shows that Jesus Christ Himself must go against our enemies, defeat them, and make us victorious. Hebron had to be His dwelling place because David in whom He was, lived there. Sin that had possessed that place must be destroyed and grace must abound there.

Judges 1:11　The Scriptures speak of the tribe of Judah as of a single man, since it points to Jesus Christ. After this mighty Conqueror has destroyed the coarsest enemies, He fights science, (Kirjath-sepher) to teach us it is a great obstacle to His reign. Learned people are very far from the Kingdom of God if they do not study the science of the saints which is that of humility, and that of constant submission to the orders of God. If they pretend to decipher the secrets of God by their science, they will always be more blind and ignorant.

Judges 1:12　Caleb knew the importance of defeating human science to be animated of divine wisdom. So he promises his daughter to whoever will destroy this city of science... Caleb had inspired the people with love and confidence when the spies were leaning on their reasoning. The daughter of Caleb is then confidence in God, by which we conquer all, and destroy our enemies.

Judges 1:13　Hope is Faith's sister. With hope comes boldness or zeal. Othniel hopes to be victorious and he is. He is therefore united to Achsah, the picture of the confidence in God. Those who trust in the Lord are never defeated.

Judges 1:14   Confidence is resting in Him Whom she trusts. She would forget everything if zeal to whom she is united did not awaken her and inspire her to ask her father for what she should have. This field is fruitfulness. How did she ask? Not with many words, persuaded that her father knows what she needs before asking... she expects everything without claiming it, and obtains more than she dared to ask.

Judges 1:15   Finally she asked a blessing. With zeal and confidence comes abandonment, and that is wonderful. Abandonment in the hands of God becomes a fertile land watered with the pure waters of grace from the everlasting hills into the low places of our humiliation and nothingness.

Judges 1:16   The city of palm trees is Jericho. It bears this name because of the most remarkable victory which ever was, of the power of God triumphant over the weakness of man. The children of the Kenite join the children of Judah, separating themselves in the wilderness, not to be corrupted by the multitude. This teaches us that we must prefer solitude, choosing Jesus and those who are most like Him.

Judges 1:17   Grace and sin can never dwell together. Sin must be entirely destroyed when we want peace in solitude. That is why Judah and Simeon slew the Canaanites. This is the work which God requires of us, doing away with sin, helped with His grace, completely. This teaches us that only Judah destroyed all the enemies of God but the other children of Israel let them live and dwelt with them. As time went by, this was the cause of all their trouble, and the entire ruin of their interior life.

Judges 1:18 As soon as we have enough courage to destroy sin, God allows many other victories.

Judges 1:19 Those who like Judah fight in Jesus Christ are given the reward of His presence and the taste of His love. Without any effort, they conquer the mountains. This means they do not have to work strenuously with their mind, God giving them through an intimate enjoyment of His presence what they could not acquire through much effort. But they could not destroy those who dwelt in the valley, which signifies that often God leaves weaknesses and defects undestroyed because they bring us into our nothingness and keep us humble before men and in our own eyes. The Scripture gives a very beautiful explanation. The inhabitants of the valley had chariots of iron. This shows that these humiliations remained to contribute to the death of ourselves.

Judges 1:20 Caleb whom we have taken to represent faith does away with the sons of Anak. They are his most opposed enemies. Faith produces confidence, abandonment, and a lack of possessiveness.

The enemies contrary to faith are distrust, and excessive care for the needs of this life, and an extraordinary attachment to these things, whether these are spiritual or natural things.

Judges 1:22 We must go against our enemies, the devil, the world and the flesh, but we must go with the Lord. This is the way to be promptly victorious. If we knew the advantage and matchless happiness we have when we walk in the presence of God, we would constantly strive to acquire this presence. God tells Abraham to do this to become perfect. David practiced it and had always the Lord before him.

Judges 1:30 These souls are surrounded by their enemies and they think they are safe because they are subject to them. They have the control over their sins but they do not get rid of them. They do not think of their sins as wild beasts which cannot be tamed and will devour them sooner or later.

Judges 1:31, 32 We see here the strange presumption of Christians who live with innumerable enemies and with as much assurance as if they were friends. How few fight these enemies and ask God for the necessary help to conquer them. We cannot be surprised if so few enjoy perfect rest in God, because this rest is acquired only by the total ruin of our enemies.

Therefore instead of fighting those who rest in the Lord because they are victorious through grace, we should rather envy them, and feel sorry for those who do not possess what is offered them through the merits of Jesus Christ, and who do not want to work at the destruction of their enemies, the strongest being their corrupt nature filled with possessiveness.

Judges 1:34 The children of Dan represent souls who free from sin want to live a more perfect life than the ordinary Christian. They live in the mountains of prayer. But there they are in a narrow place and cannot come down because of their possessiveness. If they would come down in the valley of nothingness and humility, they would find considerable room, and an extraordinary width of land.

Judges 1:35 Joseph became stronger day-by-day and conquered the least enemies. The Lord was with this tribe. The success of our perfection and our victory over our enemies depend on the presence of God with us. If our main occupation is to retain the presence of God, we will easily succeed in everything else. This suffices to become perfect since our enemies are made subject to us.

Judges 1:36 The Amorites represent self-love most perfectly because they always dwell in the highest places, corrupting what is holiest.

CHAPTER II.

Judges 2:2   God calls us to an intimate fellowship with Him. To this end we were created and redeemed. He gives a deep enjoyment of His presence to some souls. That is a sample of future bliss: but this is given only on the condition that we will be forever divorced with the enemies we spoke of in the preceding chapter. The land where we live is that of a corrupt nature. God wants us to banish its fruit, sin. Self-love is an altar that must be destroyed. This is very easy since through His blood He has delivered these enemies into our hand. But we allowed them to survive. How is that? God tells us: we did not wish to listen to His voice. Our entire happiness or misfortune depends on this. If we listen to God's voice, He instructs us on the means of doing away with these enemies. If we do not listen, we remain rebellious: our hearts harden: and He swears in His anger that we shall not enter into His rest.

Judges 2:3   This verse of Scripture is sufficient to convince us that when we are faithful in listening to His voice, keeping His alliance, being united with Him. He Himself destroys all our enemies. What are the gods of these people? They are fleshly lusts, the lusts of the eyes, and the pride of life. These are the gods that almost all men worship: they follow them, obey them: they only hear the voice of pride and of the flesh and do not know the voice of God. This is why they pitifully fall from one sin into another, and thus perish.

Judges 2:4 God warns the soul, and shows what her sin is. He warns through an angel, that is through a Servant of God, through some inspirations. He has allied Himself to this man who bears in himself the marks of this alliance which He cannot bear to destroy. Therefore He uses all kinds of means to have him return to Him, and when he repents and weeps, mourns over his wanderings, He shows him His compassions. Oh! Infinite mercy! Who would be hard enough not to surrender to You, or so insane as not to fear You?

We are all called to an union of grace and love, according to the plans of God and the faithfulness of the soul. This union stays unchangeable as far as God is concerned. However this alliance depends on one condition which is that there should be no union with the enemies which are sin and possessiveness. We all agree that we should part with the first of these enemies. . . but as for the second, we let him survive and very few let him go. He is often our friend and we are closely united to him. However, by and by this causes the ruin of our interior life. Most men are thus blinded: after sin is destroyed, they make an alliance with possessiveness. They have not allowed themselves to be completely stripped. They did not destroy certain reserves which they thought to be insignificant, and which later on cause them trouble till the end of their lives. We see such troubles in souls and we do not find the cause. They have kept that enemy which they did not believe to be dangerous and this is the main cause of these strange and painful conditions in some inner lives. Oh! Poor souls in trouble, do you not remember what you heard so often, that God is a jealous God! When these recognize their error, they weep and mourn, but it is too late. They end their lives in tears, never finding their rest which they lost by their fault. This example shows us that in each degree of perfection, some souls are more advanced than others.

Judges 2:6   When repentance is sincere, God's goodness is so great that He accepts the repentant ones. They go in peace being assured of their forgiveness and of the protection of God.

They went each one into their land. Though God has leadings common for all, there are some special for each soul. Each has an inheritance to possess, that is one's soul, and enemies to fight. The rest and enjoyment of God is the promised land for all the children of Israel, and how ever God gives each one according to one's gift and faith.

Judges 2:8, 9   Joshua possesses the rest which had been promised him, and is buried there.

The bosom of God is the place of our eternal dwelling where we are buried during all eternity. That is why the Scripture speaking of death of the saints says they die in the Lord.

Judges 2:10　All the misfortune of men comes from not knowing God, ignoring the mercies He has for those who love Him, and seek Him with their whole heart.

Judges 2:14　The most terrible result of the anger of God on man is his becoming a prey to his enemies. As soon as he withdraws from God, his strength, he becomes the victim of his enemies who bring him under subjection. He is then sold to sin not able to defend himself or to resist it.

Judges 2:17　There is an idolatry from the heart which is true prostitution. It withdraws the heart from the divine Bridegroom who acquired it at the price of His own blood to possess it and be possessed of Him. All who love unduly some creature at the expense of what they owe God are both idolaters and adulterers because they worship what they love. Paul calls covetousness an idolatry. Has Jesus Christ not said: "Where your treasure is, there is your heart also?"

Judges 2:20　Despising the goodness of God kindles the fire of His fury. He who does not burn with the sacred fire of His love will be destroyed by that of His anger. The more are the graces of God remarkable for some, the more is He insulted by the misuse of His confidence. God establishes with us an alliance for which He Himself is the reward. He asks us to do His will without any exception, to obey Him blindly, and thus He gives Himself to us. Oh! Infinite reward! Did He not say to Abraham who had obeyed him implicitly in a commandment that was harder than death: I will be your exceeding great reward? The next thing which displeases God much is when His voice is not heard. How shall we hear if we do not listen? Listening to the Lord speaking within us is the source of all good. This was David's practice. I will hear, he says, what the Lord will say to me. PS. 85:8. All evils come by not listening to God speaking within.

Judges 2:21   When God withdraws the leader that He had given us to lead us in the straight way, He Himself destroys all that would be against our progress: but if we neglect to keep His covenant, if we do not abandon ourselves to His divine will, if we do not listen to His voice in quietness and prayer, He does not make an end of our enemies. We remain under the power of our self-will, leaving the sweet freedom that comes from being subject to the will of God. Self-will is left to its own wanderings with its enemies. This is the cause of continual temptations, of these inward and violent struggles which seem so puzzling: frightful darkness comes and peace and quiet are entirely banished.

Judges 2:22   But how can God try men by things which seem to cause their loss? All work to-

13

gether for good for them that love God. Afflictions and temptations which destroy sinners through their wrong reactions will save the righteous through the right leadings of God. Only in temptation can we distinguish the righteous from sinners.

Judges 2:23 God could perfect suddenly His servants, but He does not do it. Some are sanctified by violent struggles: others are by the extreme humiliation which their depraved nature causes: and some others through continual sacrifices necessary in the circumstances in which they are. The sword of death is, in the hand of God, a fountain of life.

CHAPTER III.

Judges 3:1 The Israelites who are the people of God, led by God Himself, show perfectly the inward souls which are abandoned to the leadings of God. The rebellion of their flesh against the Spirit is an exercise of humiliation which serves to purify them of their pride, and at the same time teaches them they cannot expect much of themselves, need the protections of God, and must resort to Him. This also is an example for the majority of Christians who do not yet know the tyranny of sin and the absolute necessity to fight it, and be free early from its unbearable yoke.

Judges 3:2 The faults which remain in the perfected souls must teach the beginners the need to fight from the start relentlessly an enemy who becomes unconquerable when neglected.

Judges 3:3 These lords of the Philistines signify perfectly the rising of the flesh against the spirit and their tyrannical dominion. The Sidonians and the Hivites point to subtle sins which are the sins of the spirit and are very dangerous.

Judges 3:4 We would not have any difficulty in fulfilling the law of God if we did not have enemies preventing us from putting it into practice. In these difficulties, we give God a proof of our obedience and of our love. The greatest servants of God are tempted the most.

Judges 3:5 We have around us a multitude of enemies watching to take us by surprise. The devil is around us as a lion roaring and seeking some prey to devour. If we are not dwelling within, we will soon be devoured. But if we are shut in with God, paying attention to Him, they will not be able to hurt us. We are not supposed to fight our enemies, but we must remain quietly near God who dwells within, and this faithfulness obliges Him to put the enemies to flight.

But instead of behaving in such a pure and just way, most Christians bind themselves by criminal alliances, the causes of all trouble. They want to join together the pleasures of the flesh and the life of the Spirit, Jesus Christ and Belial, and gradually they become the servants of sin, and of the world. The devil becomes our tyrant when we give up the sweet rule of Jesus Christ.

Judges 3:7 Just as the remembrance of God is what makes us perfect, so the forgetfulness of God makes us become guilty. God is always present in the heart: and He is there to make us enjoy Him, to make us taste the sweetness of His presence. However, instead of making with Him an intact union, instead of staying within, occupied with Him, we live outwardly to offend Him in His presence.

Judges 3:8 Because of this unjust preference of the creature to the Creator, we are punished by the tyranny that this very creature exercises on us.

Judges 3:9 God gives us up to our enemies reluctantly. He allows their tyrannical empire over us just to force us to seek His help, and as soon as we do, how quickly He sends assistance! It seems He is annoyed to have to wait to be asked, and delighted to help.

Judges 3:10 This shows that those who have rule over us, have a great power from God.

Judges 3:12 The sinner repeatedly falls in his sin because he goes to sleep, stops fighting his enemies, does not live inwardly, does not shut himself with God within, under the shelter of the blows of the enemy, continually dwells in a material level, sins before God, disgraces Him, and obliges Him to strengthen some of his enemies.

Judges 3:13 When we allow some wrong to come in, and have dominion over us, quantity of other enemies unite, seeing the doors open, and find it easy to take from us the victories we had acquired through

17

the presence of Jesus Christ. It is a very sad thing to see a soul who had tasted God and the sweetness of His presence, who had walked by a quiet attention inward, becoming the prey of so many enemies because she left her God to be entertained with the vanities of the time.

Judges 3:14   The bondage of those who leave God is very long, and it is very difficult to return to God after having left Him.

Judges 3:17   Self-love is that Eglon who gets fat with all of our good works.

Judges 3:25   He who is freed from self-love is knocked down, and evil appears to be evil. Such a one appears to be such as he is.

Judges 3:27   This teaches us about the leading of a worker. He must be like Ehud who did everything right. He does not hasten Eglon's death, otherwise self-love would never be destroyed. It is very important not to rush anything, but to wait patiently the day and the moment the Lord has appointed for this defeat. But why did Ehud assemble the children of Israel after this victory which he himself had won? This shows us that if the private dealings of God are done secretly, this is not necessary for general dealings concerning all the children of God. They must be told that humiliation and nothingness are required for a perfect victory. The wise leader leads the march.

We learn that he must be the first to go down in the valley of humiliation to lead others there.

Judges 3:28   A leader like Ehud must show those he leads that God does all and not he himself. He does not say: The skill I had to kill the king makes us victorious today, but the Lord has delivered your enemies into your hands. If we follow the faithfulness of an experienced guide in the way of humility, we soon defeat what remains of our enemies.

Judges 3:29   The strongest enemies of our salvation revolve around self-love. He is their chief. A pure and right intention, a love of humility, and a lack of possessiveness are the greatest means of destroying such.

Judges 3:30   When what fed our pride is under subjection, then peace fills the soul. We have noticed up to now that peace is much longer than captivity. Eight years of captivity are followed by forty years of peace: eighteen by eighty. We thus see the great mercy of the Lord. Time to possess peace is longer than that for fighting.

CHAPTER IV.

Judges 4:1   These people withdraw from God little by little, giving up His divine leadings to govern themselves out of their pure whim, and this makes them fall into many traps.

Judges 4:2, 3   Because of this evil, God brings them under the subjection of their enemies. These represent wavering souls, spending their lives to do and undo what they have done. Sometimes they give themselves to prayer when they find someone to lead them to it, but when nothing is said about it, or they meet with some difficultly, they fall into idolatry or the love of themselves, and of their pleasure. As soon as they have left God, they find themselves subdued to their enemies. They were ruling: they become slaves. They turn again to God, and to prayer, regaining what they lost. God is ready to be merciful and He sends them help.

Judges 4:4   Deborah held then two offices which were far above a woman's task. She was a prophetess, and like Moses, she gave oracles, and made known the will of God, and she judged so great a people that Moses could not perform such a heavy charge, though he was a Godly man, and he asked for help.

We must remark that many seeing women help other women in their spiritual lives call this pride, but they are certainly mistaken because these women do so through the Spirit of God to help those that God Himself sends them in His providence, unsought for by them. They would indeed show pride if they resisted God under the pretence of humility, not submitting to His orders in complete trust. Those who refuse to help others when God's will is clear by His providence, are moved by a secret pride and self-will although they think they are humble. They either are attached to self, or are in fear of failing, or doubting divine help. They look too much to themselves. They want success in everything they do, and in the way they had expected. While the abandoned souls do not worry about succeeding or not. They leave all to God. They do not worry. They are led moment by moment by the Spirit and the will of God, speaking or being silent according to His good pleasure.

We must know that, as long as we have a desire to help souls, however small it may be, we are not very fit to do so. While we feel sweet feelings of grace speaking to others, we are not yet in the place for a pure work: the fruit will be small, accidental: but to be in the state of fruitfulness, without any mixture of self-seeking, we have no desire for anything. We speak to those sent by providence without thinking we speak. We have no feeling for anything. We are dead to any desire of helping or succeeding. We are indifferent to any occurrence. God makes us say what He wants. We cannot think of what we are going to say before speaking. Before and after speaking, we do not meditate, or reflect on what is being said. Thus are the persons called of God to help others. Acting thus they are assured of their vocation, not giving things looked for by the soul, but those given by providence.

Judges 4:5   To be dwelling under the palm tree is the sign of a settled peace which is caused by the victory over self. A woman must have a special calling from God before she can help others, and she must have perfect victory over self. . . or never attempt this. She was on Mount Ephraim which means meekness. Meekness is extremely necessary for this work. She was between Bethel and Ramah, which shows she was perfectly balanced to render justice, and free from natural desires. Deborah's seat shows she was victorious over all her enemies, and that she did not claim victory for herself, but conferred it to God, because she was not sitting on the palms as do the victorious ones, but she was under the shadow of the palm trees, which shows that God was victorious in her and by her.

Judges 4:6   It is easy to see by this verse that Deborah not only judged the people of God, but that she declared His will to them. The authority with which she speaks shows that the Almighty spoke through her mouth. This is said of Jesus Christ: He

23

taught with authority. This authority is one of the results of the divine mission, and this seal is not found in those who introduce themselves into the apostolic life.

The leader chosen of God guides to Mount Tabor from the start. It is in the sweetness of sacred love that souls are introduced through prayer. Those who thus begin progress nicely. This is the spiritual milk given to children.

This wonderful woman commands the army because when God leads a person, the natural qualities are so enriched that all is made possible. How does Deborah proceed to glorify God? She chooses Barak for a leader. She does not speak of herself, but she says: The Lord, the God of Israel orders you to lead the army. Such souls can conduct the others.

Judges 4:8   Barak having heard of the eminence of Deborah's grace, and that the Lord was with her, is assured of his mission and that the Lord was with Deborah. He tells her that if she does not want to accompany him, he will not attempt to fight. Such a distrust is commendable in those who are sent in missions, and it would be good for them to be accompanied by persons filled with the Spirit of God, and to follow with humility their advices.

Judges 4:9   God takes pleasure in doing the greatest things through weak instruments, so that victory and honor will be His. Barak was not dead sufficiently and would have taken the glory of a victory which belonged to God. This is why Deborah who knew the wonders of the wisdom and ways of God warns Barak that he would have no part in the honor of the victory. This is the reason why this chief was put into the hands of a woman. O God, You are truly God and particularly jealous of your glory. It is right that it should be given You since You alone deserve it.

Deborah, after having taken the charge of a prophet and that of a judge, takes now that of captain. What will not God be able to do with an instrument which is in His hands?

Judges 4:14　Deborah wants Barak to go and meet the enemy: Hasten, she says, to abandon yourself to your God. Fighting is not to be considered since God puts your enemies in your hands. Deborah then encourages Barak, for courage is necessary not to fight with so many enemies around, trusting in God alone. Barak came down from Mount Tabor to teach us that although the sweetness of worship is to be preferred to everything we must leave it for doing God's will. When souls are courageous, God withdraws heavenly comforts, and takes them into the fight, so as to try and purify their faith.

Judges 4:16　God wants Barak to go after his enemies. This shows us that God does not defeat our enemies to make us lazy. Prayer is the sure weapon which Jesus Christ recommends. Watch and pray. To be attentive to God within, and to pray to Him continually will find us ready for the fight.

Judges 4:17   Sin is our greatest enemy... when it is chased after, it seeks a place of refuge. It attacks perfect and surrendered souls like Jael who seems to receive him, only to destroy him.

Judges 4:21   God is so jealous of His glory that He does not give Sisera even to Deborah, though she is sufficiently dead not to take what belongs to God, but He does so because of the people who could have looked up to such a generous woman in their midst. So the Lord wanting to instruct this people, and to show them that He alone destroys the enemies: He puts them to flight and gives their captain to a woman, a foreign woman, so that all should be of God. How did Jael kill Sisera? She took a big nail from her tent. A tent is a sign of rest. When David says: O Lord, how amiable are your tabernacles: it is as if he would say: How much is your rest to be desired! To love the will of God strengthens the soul in the rest of God and this is pictured by the nail. She hit it in Sisera's head, to teach us that she hit sin in its roots. She hit it to the ground and it stayed there, because sin coming from the earth remains there. Therefore, souls freed from sin are called celestial and those under sin, earthly souls.

Judges 4:23   God humbles the very one who held the children of Israel captive. O poor souls, grieving under the bondage of sin for so long and often, why do you not abandon yourselves to God, and give yourselves to Him through prayer? In no time, through divine power, you will have under your feet those who held you captive.

Judges 4:24 God's dealings with souls who are abandoned to Him appear so well in the Scriptures. He strengthens them little by little, and brings more and more under their subjection, the devil and sin. But this is done slowly because if God did this suddenly, the soul who is still weak would appropriate the glory for itself, and thus fall again. He then does all things little by little on account of the weakness of the creature, and at last He entirely destroys its enemies, and gives true peace. But there is much to suffer, although this cannot be compared to the bondage of sin.

God, in His entire dealings with this people, has wanted to show us that as soon as we withdraw from Him, wanting to be free, we fall under bondage. These people were captured when they went into idolatry. But when they acknowledged their mistake coming back under the leadings of God, they were delivered and made victorious over those who held them down. Man's unfaithfulness and changes are used to show in a better way the faithfulness and goodness of God.

CHAPTER V.

Judges 5:1-3   Who are those who can and must sing this song? Those who distinguished themselves from the rest. How? In offering themselves willingly at the peril of their lives, not sparing anything with God when His will and glory were at stake. This is supported by these words of the Lord: "Whosoever will save his life shall lose it: and whosoever will lose his life for my sake shall find it." This shows that true salvation involves the loss of any earthly attachment. God wants a willing sacrifice.

We must draw the conclusion that there is no risk in abandoning ourselves to God. He is never defeated by a loving deed. The more we risk for Him, the greater salvation and perfection we find in Him.

Judges 5:5   This shows that the mountains of the highest knowledge disappear before God, and that what was acquired vanishes away. This is far from being a loss: it is a gain, because it is the sign that the God of Israel Himself comes. Nothing can survive before Him. Instead of being grieved by this, we must say with Saint Paul: "What things were gain to me, those I counted loss for Christ."

This also can explain what happens to the converted sinner. When God appears to give life to this sinner, his accumulated crimes which seemed to be mountains vanish away, and no traces remain.

Judges 5:6 Sinners before their conversion allow the highways of righteousness to take a rest. They walk in the unoccupied byways, running in the path of iniquity.

Judges 5:7 How did she get up? She did so, that she could be a mother and bring to life again this people of God. All those who have gone thus far possess the qualities of a mother. It seems they carry in their bosom the souls they watch over through the graces which they impart to them. They lead them and love them as do true mothers.

Judges 5:10 It is proper that they who are riding on white donkeys should speak of the marvels of God. What does this mean? Simply this, that those in whom God has through His power destroyed all their enemies, are now above their nature which is purified, and have become white in the blood of the Lamb. They are riding because the purified flesh is brought under subjection to the Spirit. These are also sitting in judgment, publishing the praises of the Lord on account of the perfect rest they enjoy through an entire confidence in Him who did all in them and for them.

Judges 5:16 The Spirit of God, through Deborah utters a complaint and a correction for the souls who are not entirely given to Him, and who abandon themselves half-heartedly like Reuben. They are divided against themselves to God, and they fear they will have to lose sight of themselves, and will also lose visible helps on which they lean. They give themselves and withdraw themselves, abandoning themselves for one thing and not for the other. They go thus far and no further. This divided heart holds them throughout their lives in unexplainable torments. We think this is given of God when in fact, it just comes by resisting Him. God draws and wants the soul to be lost in Him. The creature withholds and suffers unbearable martyrdom simply because of not being entirely God's or wholly in self.

CHAPTER VI.

Judges 6:2 The Scripture describes beautifully here the condition of a soul who having tasted the happiness of the presence of God has just left Him, forgotten Him and lost the practice of His presence. Little by little, the enemies whom God had subdued, out of sheer kindness, become the masters. Since God does not want to lose the soul He favored with such an eminent grace which is that of having tasted the goodness of the Lord, He permits her enemies to attack her furiously so that she does not know where to hide. She hides in the caves of the mountains, trying to gain by meditation and the examples of the saints. She finds a refuge in the strongholds of strict living to resist such powerful enemies, but alas: having left the inward refuge of the soul, she is hunted by her enemies.

Judges 6:3, 4 A soul which is deprived of an inner life is like an open vineyard, exposed to all kinds of plunderings, while a soul hiding with God inwardly is an unconquerable fort, holding her shelter in spite of the efforts of her enemies. All the virtuous acts of the outward souls are like good seed, but they are spoiled by that crowd of strange enemies which bind her to the things of the world, possessions, honors, and continual life of outwardness.

Judges 6:7-10   Those who leave their inner life after having tasted God are always overwhelmed and oppressed, and since they have tasted the sweetness of His love, being tired of their captivity, they run back to Him. They cry out, which is a sign of a sincere repentance. They ask for help, realizing they must not expect any from themselves. God immediately sends some enlightened person who shows them that the cause of their whole trouble came simply in forsaking their inner life by which they always could hear the voice of God.

God's reproaches are full of strength and kindness. "Did I not deliver you," says God, "from the captivity of your sins, and even from outward activity and growth? I drove away your most dangerous enemies, and made you possess your soul in peace. I told you: I am the Lord your God, dwelling always with you, if you want to be with Me. Do not fear. But you have not listened to My voice, although it was within you."

Judges 6:11   When, like Gideon, we are busy threshing wheat, that is, meditating on His Word to hold it within, and thus hide it from the enemies of our salvation, we will not fail to find favor with God, and to receive His protection.

Judges 6:12 The greatest grace that God can bestow upon a soul who seeks Him is to manifest Himself to that one. As soon as we apply our heart to meditate on the Word of the Lord, and to retain it, God does not fail to send us somebody with this wonderful news that the Lord is with us. O wondrous bliss, fount of all blessing for a soul strengthened by this divine presence. The Angel calls Gideon a mighty man of valor, to show us that man's strength lies in the study of God's Word. Human action cannot go beyond this. Those who do this try to reach the goal, while the rest are engaged in amusements, being in earthly things.

Judges 6:13 The Angel had told Gideon that the Lord was with him, but he had not told him He was with the rest of the people. Nevertheless, Gideon answers as if they all were included. This shows Gideon's humility, and also his understanding that if God is for us, we cannot be under the bondage of our enemies. It is impossible for God not to protect those He honors with His presence.

Judges 6:14 When the Lord looks upon a man, a communication of His Word is taking place. Mary expresses it this way in her song: "He hath regarded the low estate of His handmaiden." In this way He enables him to do everything.

Judges 6:15 The man who is humble but alive in himself refuses the divine mission judging himself unworthy. Active virtue goes thus far. But the man who is dead to self offers no resistance because he does not expect anything of himself. He knows that God does not need any strength of our own to fulfill His designs and His will. He is self-sufficient. So the weakest instrument serves His purposes as well as the strongest.

Judges 6:16-17   However weak we may be, as soon as the Lord is with us, we have sufficient strength. But to show that there is no real humility except through a real death to self, Gideon's humility is changed into distrust, and asks for signs. He who is truly humble, dead to self, obeys blindly, without a word because he is not looking for any success. He is equally satisfied to be defeated or to win. He only thinks of obeying. Others want certainties because they do not wish to have the embarrassment of a daring undertaking. But what greater certainty can we have than that of having God with us? All else is below this, and we make a mistake by wanting something else.

Judges 6:18-20   Gideon wants to prepare a sacrifice that will nourish the Angel. Everyone who is active proceeds likewise. Through their reasoning power they prepare and get things ready for the Lord, and thus they think they will please Him. But they are taught that the true sacrifice is that of nothingness, pouring out one's heart before the Lord, and allowing it to be consumed by the fire of His love.

Judges 6:21, 22   Active persons are surprised

and frightened by the least extraordinary things which happen to them. Moses is not surprised to see God face to face, and Gideon is frightened by an Angel.

Judges 6:23 The Lord Himself gives peace. True visions always give peace to the soul, but that peace, like the vision itself, is passing. There is nothing to fear because while lights are maintained, death to self never occurs.

Judges 6:25 The bullock is a picture of strength. God teaches us that we must use the strength of our zeal for the members of our family to whom we are the most indebted, before going to others. Paul wanted the deacons to be examined in this respect. We also learn that in such questions as self-denial, we must begin in our own lives, and that the true messenger will not lay on others a yoke he has not first taken.

Judges 6:26 Gideon is instructed that he must offer sacrifices to God alone, and not to the Angel. This teaches us that we must overlook the gifts and return to the Giver, staying with Him only.

Judges 6:27 As much as it is possible, we should hide good works, for fear that self-love, and presumption would make them worthless.

Judges 6:29 As soon as (through a special leading of the Holy Spirit), we work at the destruction of self-love within us or in others, we should expect persecution, because to this idol, most men sacrifice.

Judges 6:31   We see that although the servants of the Lord are persecuted for a lapse of time, God protects them in a singular way, while He takes vengeance on those who dishonor Him sooner or later, although they may prosper for a while.

Judges 6:34-38   The Spirit of the Lord came upon Gideon as a garment only, because he was still occupied with powerful means, and so the Spirit of God was not given him by infusion. Some receive the Spirit through their center, and others in powerful means and in their senses. Therefore Gideon asks for a sign and a witness from God. When it pleases God to use souls leaning on lights to help others, they need a number of assurances and tangible witnesses. The goodness of God must be very great to bear with such creatures in their weakness, for can there be something more insulting to God than believing an imperfect witness rather than His word? However most people make this mistake. They prefer weak witnesses which do not amount to anything, and where there is much deception, to the pure and naked faith which is a hidden and efficacious word from God. Nevertheless, for God to condescend to the weakness of these people grants them very often what they desire, so as to stir them to do what He wants them to do.

Judges 6:39   These souls are not satisfied with one witness. They need several because they only

only act with assurances, while the souls that are moved by faith only need this unique support, and faith is their whole certitude in the midst of uncertainties. Faith is great when the more witnesses lack, the more assured we are without assurances.

CHAPTER VII.

Judges 7:1, 2 The people that Gideon had with him was a wonderful picture of the multitude of gifts, graces, favors, lights, witnesses, virtues, strength, in one's self, in the natural and supernatural talents with which these kinds of souls are loaded and filled. God makes Gideon understand that all these crowds will not defeat the enemies. It is not by the might of man that victory is won. And why, O my God? He says it Himself: It is "lest Israel vaunt themselves against Me."

Judges 7:3 God commands the fearful souls to withdraw because they apprehend the loss of their created gifts very strongly. Those who hold on to them are not fit for the Lord's work.

Judges 7:4 You find there are too many with the ten thousand that remain: Yes, they are too many because they must be tried at the water of affliction and bitterness. How few will go through this trial which is the loss of all they held tight and on which they rested.

Judges 7:5 "Every one that boweth down upon his knees" is a wonderful picture of many who are resting on all kinds of apparent and spiritual delights. These are not fit for the work of the Lord because they stop with everything they meet, rest there, and never go forward, instead of going beyond, as do those who use these apparent and spiritual delights only when necessary. These are very well designated as "lapping of the water as a dog lappeth," without bending their knees, nor stopping resting for a moment at these things, for kneeling and resting show the delight they are taking.

Judges 7:13, 14 The Scripture interprets this dream. Gideon is the bread, not of good and strong wheat, but of coarse barley. However, having lost quickly strange help, and much support, God will deliver all his enemies into his hands... such bread cooked with coals and thrown to the ground is a picture of humiliation.

Judges 7:15,16 When Gideon heard the dream, he knew the mystery of nothingness. He worshipped before the deep secrets of righteousness and mercy. They were given empty pitchers. This emptiness refers to the nothingness of the soul by the loss of its powers. These pitchers made of earth represent the weakness of our nature and also nature itself, hiding divine virtues. The lamps that are lit in the pitchers clearly show the charity which though hidden in the weakness of nature is burning strong. They also have trumpets which are as a voice given to publish from the depth of their miseries the power and the righteousness of God.

Judges 7:17, 18   If we wish to look at Gideon for a moment, and draw a parallel between him and Moses, it will be easy to differentiate them by this single passage. Moses who was purified and utterly emptied of self never appears in whatever he does, however great it may be. He gives all to God, and does not share His glory. But Gideon wants to be mentioned in the victory, which is a very great mistake. However God who stoops to the weakness of these souls seems not to pay any attention to it, makes use of it to save His people, while He punishes Moses very severely for his mistake near the rock though it was much smaller. O God, you tolerate, it seems, big defects in souls which you call to an ordinary perfection only, whereas you punish with an extreme harshness a light mistake in a soul you take pleasure in.

Judges 7:19-22   There are hardly any places in the Holy Scriptures which prove better than this the weakness of the creature and the power of God enclosed in this creature: neither is there any which make us understand better that we are not indebted to our strength for the defeat of our enemies, but to the goodness of God. How does He destroy our enemies? He wants these three hundred men to break their pitchers and to blow their trumpets. This teaches us that charity is always imprisoned in us, though victorious, until the pitcher, our nature, is broken. Nothingness must break this pitcher so that charity will be seen in its brightness and warmth. Paul expresses it so well when he says that we bear this treasure in earthen vessels, so that the excellency of the power will be of God, and not of us.

Why are these men blowing the trumpets? This is to teach us that the true result of charity will always be a complete satisfaction in God, no matter how He deals with us.

CHAPTER VIII.

Judges 8:1   We saw in Moses a man chosen of God to be a leader of the people. God communicated Himself to Moses face-to-face, essence-to-essence, this being the most sublime condition in which God can call a soul, and the highest communication that God makes of Himself.

Gideon walked on a path full of light. He advanced little, and had no higher communication than by powerful means. We saw the difference in the leadings of Moses and of Gideon, and the difference in their death. Moses was always careful not to claim God's graces as his own. He was chosen to help souls, and prepared for this in a superior way. Though he was faithful, he made a mistake in behalf of the people which did not bring him down from his attainments, but which stopped him from leading the people to their ultimate end. And this mistake was necessary to the glory of God, if we may thus express ourselves, so that nothing would be conferred to Moses' strength. This might have happened it he had led the people to the end. God had to make these people know that

His power was confined in Himself, independently from the creature who is made to share this power as He pleases. Otherwise this uncouth people would have made an idol of Moses, ascribing to him the power that belonged to God alone. Joshua is also included with Moses, though his perfection is somewhat lesser. Gideon is different. He is with those whom God takes in the way of beginners in order to help others, and who will do so only with witnesses and lights, claiming for themselves the power they are given, or at least part of it. And this claim is the ruin of their inner life, and the loss of their progress, though they retain their salvation.

Chapter XIII.

Judges 13:7, 14   We find another difference in Samson. He must abstain from many things,
so that he is a fine example of Godly people who rely
in their holy ways. Although their strength is well
known, it destroys very few enemies, as we will soon
see. The personal holiness of such a person has never
been so well expressed. When one's strength is in
doing and thinking, this being referred to by the hair,
great care must be taken not to cut them or remove
them, because the strength which is in that would
be lost.

CHAPTER XIV.

Judges 14:5, 6   The first enemy that these kind of persons have to fight is the devil who like a roaring lion seeks whom he may devour. They are victorious at first by the strength of the Spirit of the Lord coming upon them, and they rent and chase the devil like they would a fly. These souls often struggle with the enemy and come out victorious. They are strengthened and established in holiness.

Judges 14:14   We understand this to refer to the active person who is feeding and sustained by good deeds out of which spring words nourishing those who hear them. These are very strong through grace from which comes forth sweetness, a great blessing to others according to the plan of God.

Chapter XV.

Judges 15:5   All Samson does is promoted by zeal and a fervor in which self-interest is mixed, and though God uses this to the destruction of his enemies, it is very imperfect. So these obvious spoils, and striking wonders only hurt the fruit, hindering his enemy from gathering his crop, but this enemy was not destroyed.

Judges 15:10,11   As soon as the devil is attacked in his stronghold, his havoc is greater, and not being able to touch the shepherd, he goes after the flock. The inward ones feel the new attacks of the enemy, and are grieved. They are perplexed. When temptation comes to them, they rise against their leader.

Judges 15:13   The leader must have enough love to do what these weak souls want, excluding sin. It is sometimes well to accept being brought up from the rock, like Samson, not standing firm by what is more perfect, so as to strengthen the weak, deigning to be gracious.

Judges 15:14   If the leader must stoop to the weakness of the weak, God never fails to help him in time of need.   There is no bond that is strong enough to stand against the Spirit of God.   Only the bondage of sin remaining in a rebellious will cannot be broken by God.

Judges 15:15   What is most evil and earthly is often used in the hands of a qualified worker to destroy our enemies.   God makes everything work for good to them who love Him.

Judges 15:16   If Samson had been humble, he would not have claimed this victory for himself. Here is the difference between souls that are strong in themselves and those that are devoid of themselves, the first ascribe their victories to their talent, and the others think it is their duty to refer them to God.

Judges 15:18   Samson who has just defeated so many enemies is sore athirst.   Those who like David fight in God, and glory in God, do not feel thirsty because they are drinking from the spring-water. We must have a strong sense of nothingness not to feel thirsty anymore.   Some are thirsty for honors, pleasures, at least for spiritual things.   We often suffer bareness because we try to quench our thirst away from God, and we have not like David a single thirst which is that of the living God.

Judges 15:19   Why is it not said of him, like of others, that the Lord was with him?   This is to show us that with him everything was worked out in a lively, distinct, and extraordinary way. So water is given him, as a reward, that is, much comfort. But where does this water come from? Not from Heaven but from the very means which was used to destroy his enemies. This first shows that the comfort was obvious, then it was in thinking and claiming for one's self the thing that was worked out in a miraculous way. Those who are perfected never think of what God works out in them or through them. In this way, they have no outward comfort. However this comfort is necessary to imperfect souls. Through them they renew their strength which is knocked down by the least dryness. This prevents them from fainting.

Judges 15:20   How is it that the Scripture says that Samson judged Israel in the days of the Philistines, and that it does not say, like for the other judges, that God delivered the people from the oppression of their enemies, and also that this people enjoyed peace? This makes us to understand that the leader or the judge cannot lead a soul in a higher and stronger way than he is led himself. A man living in self, and not entirely free from himself, cannot free others, neither can he teach them a way that he does not know, while he who is free from earthly desires can alone show the proper way to set others free. These active persons, though they are strong doing good, never lead to perfect freedom.

CHAPTER XVI.

Judges 16:1   After such miraculous deeds, Samson's fall is strange. This teaches us that while we stay in self, we can fall from the highest summit of perfection to the greatest wretchedness.

Judges 16:2   As soon as the enemy of our salvation hears that the servants of God venture in ways that will offend God, he has a great joy. Though he does not confound them first in their spiritual life, he is certain that they will, sooner or later, fall into his traps. The clear proof of this is in what follows of Samson's life. Truly the devil walketh about, as a roaring lion, seeking whom he may devour. He watches when we sleep. That is why it is so important not to go into the sleep of sin, and to watch with God so that God will watch over us.

Judges 16:3   As soon as Samson arises, he does miraculous works like those of his first strength.

Judges 16:5   As soon as we set our heart against the will of God, and give it to the creature to the hurt of what we owe God, the devil is sure to win a full victory, for where your treasure is, there will your heart be also. If our heart is in God, our treasure is in God alone, but if our heart is the creature's, we become this creature's idolaters. He who recklessly exposes himself to danger, will perish there. We must leave all for God, and lose all to gain Him, even our own life, according to the advice of the Gospel.

What the enemy of our soul wants to know most is "wherein our strength lieth," so as to know it straight to the point. Each saint has always had a special virtue in which he excelled. For some, it was humility, for others, charity, for these, the sacrificial spirit, and for those, the abandonment of themselves in the hands of God. The devil aims only at this strong-hold. The arrangement of the inward life depends on this. When an abandoned soul leaves her abandon-ment, she loses her balance, even if she would ex-hibit a multitude of other virtues.

Judges 16:6   The devil uses the creatures we idolize to find out what hinders us in becoming his slaves. He wants to know how he may bind us. Sad to say, he will know it too soon. Resisting so weakly will help to make us fall shamefully into the trap with great hurt.

Judges 16:16   After undertaking our loss, and having a hold on us, the devil seeks all the most suitable ways to succeed in his plans. Usually he suc-ceeds in giving no rest to the heart and mind, filling them continually, and especially in taking away the rest of prayer. As soon as we lose prayer, we are certain to fall into the trap of the enemy. Prayer is the food of the soul. In this sacred rest, the soul takes its needed strength. Deprive it of this food, it will right away fall into a swoon, and often a deadly swoon.

Judges 16:17 Three times had Samson experienced Delilah's betrayals. Nevertheless he declares to her a secret that he should have silenced at any cost. A man who is consecrated to God from youth is not for this reason sheltered from falls. If he kept all of his desires for God, his strength would last indefinitely. But the razor of profane love takes them away and he becomes the weakest of men.

Judges 16:18 The treason of this woman is strange. For money she betrays the one who loves her into the hands of his most deadly enemies. Most women sacrifice their love to their interest. The love of money is so strong that it rises above love itself which no other love can shake. Only you, O my God, love man freely, and this ungrateful man does not repay you with a grateful love.

Judges 16:19 In this manner we allow ourselves to go to sleep in enchanting pleasures. When we think we rest on a loving heart, we rest on Delilah, our most dangerous enemy.

Samson's example teaches us that whatever strength a virtuous man may have, he may fall in a moment, and become the weakest of men. However his weaknesses are profitable because they deprive him of the strength he had in himself. All of Samson's misfortune came in claiming for himself what God did for him. God allows his strength to be destroyed to instruct him by his experience of all he would do without the help of grace. Only through our mistakes are we perfectly taught.

Judges 16:20   Samson thought he was strong and he was weak. We are often ignorant of our capacities, and we think we can do what we did formerly, like Samson who did mighty wonders while the Spirit of the Lord stayed with him, but since the Lord forsook him, he falls in real weakness.

The Scripture is wonderful in its expressions. It says that "he knew not that the Lord was departed from him." When we recklessly go in paths of sin, we think we will always come out victoriously as long as we think we are full of strength, but the Lord irritated by rashness forsakes us and we fall in weakness. Blessed are those, Lord, whom You never forsake, and of whom can always be said: "The Lord is with them."

Judges 16:21   Here is a very exact description of the condition where we are brought by sin. From victorious life, we become captive. Samson who had dominion over the Philistines has been made their slave, and is bound with fetters. Samson, what happened to your strength, and courage? You, who destroyed the Philistines with the jawbone of an ass, are grinding in your prison like an ass! You subdued everybody, and now you are bound! He who judged Israel, and was chosen of God to free them from their enemies is brought into subjection by these very enemies!

First they put out his eyes. The first result of sin is to darken the eyes of our understanding. Then we are bound with chains which become heavier every day. But serving the Lord we become freer daily. In God our heart is enlarged, and in sin the prison is more narrow every day. In short, the yoke of the Lord is easy, and His burden is light, and the yoke of sin is very troublesome.

Judges 16:24 Nothing satisfies so much the devil than the victory he wins on the servants of the Lord. Just as in heaven there is great joy over the conversion of a sinner, even so in hell there is a great joy over the fall of a true servant of God. But if God permits His servants to be humiliated by their falls, He does not allow them to be lost for this. He raises them after having humbled them to excess.

Judges 25-28 If Samson is their toy for a moment, he will soon take his revenge. When God withdrew from him, he fell in weakness, and death. But as soon as he calls on the Lord, he is brought back in his first strength. Lord, You delight in allowing your children to fall so that they will come to You again for help, just like a father will let his son fall to have him come for help and protection.

SeedSowers

P.O. Box 3317
Jacksonville, FL 32206
800-228-2665
904-598-3456 (fax)   www.seedsowers.com

REVOLUTIONARY BOOKS ON CHURCH LIFE

The House Church Movement *(Begier, Richey, Vasiliades, Viola)* 9.95
How to Meet In Homes *(Edwards)* 10.95
An Open Letter to House Church Leaders *(Edwards)* 4.00
When the Church Was Led Only by Laymen *(Edwards)* 4.00
Beyond Radical *(Edwards)* 5.95
Rethinking Elders *(Edwards)* 9.95
Revolution, The Story of the Early Church *(Edwards)* 8.95
The Silas Diary *(Edwards)* 9.99
The Titus Diary *(Edwards)* 8.99
The Timothy Diary *(Edwards)* 9.99
The Priscilla Diary *(Edwards)* 9.99
The Gaius Diary *(Edwards)* 10.99
Overlooked Christianity *(Edwards)* 14.95

AN INTRODUCTION TO THE DEEPER CHRISTIAN LIFE

Living by the Highest Life *(Edwards)* 8.99
The Secret to the Christian Life *(Edwards)* 8.99
The Inward Journey *(Edwards)* 8.99

CLASSICS ON THE DEEPER CHRISTIAN LIFE

Experiencing the Depths of Jesus Christ *(Guyon)* 8.95
Practicing His Presence *(Lawrence/Laubach)* 8.95
The Spiritual Guide *(Molinos)* 8.95
Union With God *(Guyon)* 8.95
The Seeking Heart *(Fenelon)* 9.95
Intimacy with Christ *(Guyon)* 10.95
Spiritual Torrents *(Guyon)* 10.95
The Ultimate Intention *(Fromke)* 11.00

IN A CLASS BY THEMSELVES

The Divine Romance *(Edwards)* 8.95
The Story of My Life as told by Jesus Christ *(Four gospels blended)* 14.95
Acts in First Person *(Book of Acts)* 9.95

COMMENTARIES BY JEANNE GUYON

Genesis Commentary 10.95
Exodus Commentary 10.95
Leviticus - Numbers - Deuteronomy Commentaries 12.95
Judges Commentary 7.95
Job Commentary 10.95
Song of Songs *(Song of Solomon Commentary)* 9.95
Jeremiah Commentary 7.95
James - I John - Revelation Commentaries 12.95

THE CHRONICLES OF THE DOOR *(Edwards)*

The Beginning 8.99
The Escape 8.99
The Birth 8.99
The Triumph 8.99
The Return 8.99

THE WORKS OF T. AUSTIN-SPARKS

The Centrality of Jesus Christ 19.95
The House of God 29.95
Ministry 29.95
Service 19.95
Spiritual Foundations 29.95
The Things of the Spirit 10.95
Prayer 14.95
The On-High Calling 10.95
Rivers of Living Water 8.95
The Power of His Resurrection 8.95

COMFORT AND HEALING

A Tale of Three Kings *(Edwards)* 8.99
The Prisoner in the Third Cell *(Edwards)* 5.99
Letters to a Devastated Christian *(Edwards)* 7.95
Healing for those who have been Crucified by Christians *(Edwards)* 8.95
Dear Lillian *(Edwards)* 5.95

OTHER BOOKS ON CHURCH LIFE

Climb the Highest Mountain *(Edwards)* 9.95
The Torch of the Testimony *(Kennedy)* 14.95
The Passing of the Torch *(Chen)* 9.95
Going to Church in the First Century *(Banks)* 5.95
When the Church was Young *(Loosley)* 8.95

CHRISTIAN LIVING

The Autobiography of Jeanne Guyon 14.95
Final Steps in Christian Maturity *(Guyon)* 12.95
Turkeys and Eagles *(Lord)* 8.95
The Life of Jeanne Guyon *(T.C. Upham)* 17.95
Life's Ultimate Privilege *(Fromke)* 10.00
Unto Full Stature *(Fromke)* 10.00
All and Only *(Kilpatrick)* 7.95
Adoration *(Kilpatrick)* 8.95
Release of the Spirit *(Nee)* 6.00
Bone of His Bone *(Huegel)* *modernized* 8.95

*call for a free catalog 800-228-2665